Paul *Young*

John Merrill

BOBCAT BOOKS

LONDON · NEW YORK · SYDNEY · COLOGNE

© Copyright 1986 Omnibus Press Bobcat Books
(A Division Of Book Sales Limited)

Art Direction by: Mike Bell
Co-ordination by: Lynda Hassett
Book design by: Mainartery
Picture research by: Valerie Boyd

ISBN: 0.7119.0785.4
Order No: OP 43611

Exclusive distributors:
Book Sales Limited,
78 Newman Street, London W1P 3LA, UK.
Omnibus Press,
GPO Box 3304, Sydney, NSW 2001,
Australia.

To the Music Trade only:
Music Sales Limited,
78 Newman Street, London W1P 3LA, UK.

Picture credits:
London Features International Ltd,
Barry Plummer, Retna Pictures Ltd,
Rock Photos

Typeset by Capital Setters
Printed in Great Britain by Blantyre Printing
& Binding Limited, Blantyre, Glasgow.

A milling crowd of girls stand around outside the offices of CBS Records in London's Soho Square. Through the plate glass doors a security guard hovers, eyeing the mob nervously and awaiting the moment when the crush threatens his own territory. He's been through all this before; a couple of years ago it was Adam Ant, before that David Essex. Next year and it'll most likely be someone else.

Behind the crowd, a limousine pulls up, its engine purring to a halt. An expectant hush falls over the crowd, broken only when the rear door opens to reveal a middle aged man, short and balding, impeccably dressed. An executive.

Disinterestedly the crowd parts a little; happy to let the man past, reluctant to give up their little patch closest to the door. The security man waits a moment, then steps forward to allow the executive entry. Immediately several pairs of hands grab the door and hold it open.

"Is Paul coming in today?" Both men glance at the speaker, a girl. "Paul Young," she explains patiently. "Will he be in today?"

P a u l   Y o u n g

The security man shrugs. He knows from past experience it doesn't matter what he says. The girls will stay here all day regardless. And tomorrow they'll be back. Tomorrow and the next day, and the day after that. And then they'll get fed up and go off to wait for somebody else. Pop fans are like that. Smilingly he closes the door and returns to his post by the desk.

But every so often a pop star comes along who isn't simply a 15 minute wonder, someone whose career doesn't revolve around a handful of hits and a few walls of dog-eared posters. Whose talent will not burn out, whose career cannot be measured in the amount of time it takes for their records to get from the pressing plant to the bargain bins. Somebody who, quite simply, is a phenomenon.

One such phenomenon hit British radio in June, 1983. It burst into a chart overladen with disco drivel and tired old rockers, a precocious originality which was blended with a stroke of brilliant timing.

To a few people, the song was already familiar. "Wherever I Lay My Hat" was written and recorded by Marvin Gaye back in 1963. To other folk, the artist rang a few bells as well. Paul Young was already renowned as one-time singer with Q-Tips, a band whose sparkling reworkings of the soul hits of the 1960s made them one of the biggest attractions ever to hit the club circuit. Neither song nor artist had been particularly successful in chart terms in the past, but together they made for a combination that was unbeatable.

The story began at the end of May, when the *New Musical Express* elected "Wherever I Lay My Hat" its single of the week. Just seven days later, the song had pushed its way into the Top 75. Within three weeks it was poised just outside the Top 10. Three weeks after that, it was number 1.

LIFE SAVING   RATUS

Paul Young makes an unlikely star. Quiet and withdrawn, he chooses his words almost as carefully as he chooses the songs he records. Any image he projects is totally natural to him, one over which he has total control. Whereas so many of today's – and yesterday's – top artists are manipulated to such a degree that they are little more than puppets for their backers to play with, Paul has been at least partially responsible for every major decision of his career so far. It was

he who selected the members of his band, he who chose the name, defying even his record company who insisted that The Royal Family would be far better suited to a punk band. Paul even designed the family crest which was to be the backdrop for his stage appearances. He has only himself to thank for the efforts which conspired to bring him the acclaim he had been searching for, yet typically down to earth, he regards that acclaim with nothing short of bemusement.

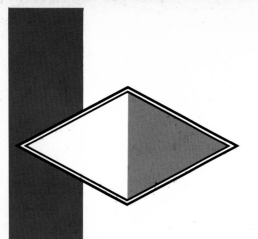

"I was so shocked when 'Wherever I Lay My Hat' went into the Top 30," he has said. "I just kept refusing to believe it. When it got to number 12 I thought 'I don't want it to go to number 1'. I really didn't. I was saying to my manager: 'Can't you ask them to stop pressing the record or something?' I don't want a career that is going to burn out in a few months. I want something steady."

Paul's fears were well founded. There is no counting the number of artists who have burst on to the scene in a blaze of publicity and sky high sales, only to sink back into obscurity as soon as their next record comes out. But such was not to be a problem for Paul. A succession of television appearances, ranging from Top Of The Pops to Saturday Superstore and back again, kept him visible enough for people to grow aware of him, but not so much that they reached for the off switch every time his face appeared on the screen. Everything was timed impeccably.

"Come Back And Stay", Paul's next single, was released just as his first solo tour got under way, climbing the chart even as the tour snaked its way round the country. "Love Of The Common People", a single originally released to total apathy a year before, was reactivated at the beginning of December, riding high on the traditional pre-Christmas sales boom.

"No Parlez", the album from which all three singles were taken, was in the chart for over a year without a break. At the last count, sales were approaching seven million copies worldwide. "The Secret Of Association", Paul's second LP released early in 1985, has done almost as well, in only half the time! And then there have been the tours, massively successful both at home and abroad. Taken all together, there can be little wonder that Paul's name is now almost as well known and loved as that of the Royal Family after whom he named his band.

Yet for all the millions of words said and written about him, Paul remains a very private person. Fame is not the be all and end all of life for him; you do not find him cavorting about the media circus so beloved by his chart topping contemporaries. His is not a face which you find staring out of your newspaper every morning, forever linked with headline hungry starlets or a fracas in some exclusive nightclub. His comings and goings are not splashed across front pages, his offstage life is not conducted beneath the glare of a thousand flashbulbs. He consents to interviews only when there is something to be interviewed about. In his own words, he is just a singer of songs, a persona which, in the 1980s, might seem a little outmoded. As one American critic wrote: "He doesn't dress like a woman. He doesn't hide behind a wall of synthesizers. He wasn't inspired by the punk movement of 1976. What *does* he have going for him?"

*   *   *   *

Paul Anthony Young was born on January 17th, 1956, at Grove Road Maternity Home in Luton. His parents, Doris and Tony, already had one son, Mark. He grew up with as much awareness of music as any child of his age – the first record he ever bought was "Riders On The Storm" by The Doors. Slade were the first group he ever saw in concert, and "Fire And Water", by Free, was the starting point in what is now a huge and varied LP collection.

"Free was a great band," Paul said later. "They had a lot of soul and Paul Rodgers had a tremendous feel to his voice. I never saw Free live, but I just loved the records... the sound of Rodgers' voice. That's what made me want to be a singer. I wanted to be a singer like him, but nobody seemed impressed. In the end I copied Andy Fraser, gave up my piano lessons and took up bass instead."

It was always Rodgers who influenced Paul the most, however. Seven years older than Paul, he had been singing in blues bands since his teens, cultivating one of the most distinctive and powerful voices in rock. In interviews he would always cite soul singers like Otis Redding as his major inspiration and, as Paul's interest grew, he too began to explore these roots.

Paul Young

"I really studied Otis," Paul said. "When he was born, when he died. I read everything I could get my hands on." He followed Redding's own lead and picked up on another great soul vocalist, Sam Cooke; today, Paul rates Cooke alongside Otis and Marvin Gaye as having "an almost perfect soul voice. It's really sweet, but he turns on that nice bit of roughness at the top." Cooke's 1959 album, "Encore", is one of Paul's most treasured possessions.

Working days at the Vauxhall car factory in Luton, Paul played in local bands after he left school. He quickly discovered a glut of bass players in the area, so he gave up that instrument and returned to his first love, singing. Immediately he ran into problems of a different kind. Paul was already aware that soul music was not particularly popular amongst his friends – they were all into heavy metal and Paul used to hide his Stevie Wonder albums every time somebody visited him. At the first audition he ever tried, it was a friend who landed the job "because he had the Robert Plant look and threw all the right shapes with his hair".

Paul Young

Paul did find some work, however. One of his earliest bands, Kat Kool & The Kool Kats, became a popular band on the local circuit, building up a huge following before going their separate ways in 1977. And Paul, with one eye still on the adulation which he received with that band, and the other focused sharply on the suddenly emergent Punk Rock, lost very little time in hitching up with another unit.

Street Band was based in north London and, besides Paul, included guitarists Roger Kelly and John Gifford, bassist Mick Pearl and drummer Vince Chaulk, a former member of Mr. Big whose "Romeo" had been one of the biggest hits of 1977.

Street Band immediately set themselves apart from the majority of other
new bands playing the London circuit.
Their music was several steps removed
from the cut and thrust tactics of the more
"committed" punk bands. In Roger Kelly
they had one of the country's most
exciting young guitarists. Their attempts
at songwriting harkened back to the
heydays of 10cc and Gary Holton's Heavy
Metal Kids. And Paul, when he let rip,
had one of the finest singing voices
around. Small wonder, then, that Street
Band was barely six months old before
they won a record contract.

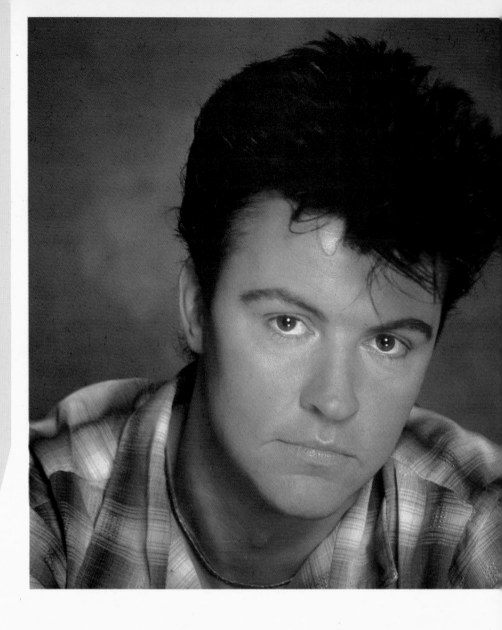

a   *u*   *l*

If their approach to musicianship was a cut above the fashionable incompetent norm, then Street Band's attitude towards live work was positively eccentric. They ignored established venues such as the Roxy and the Marquee, instead taking bookings in pubs and clubs where they would appear alongside Irish folk bands and aspiring country and western singers performing Frank Sinatra's greatest hits. It was a move which gave the group plenty of opportunity to build up their own following, as well as polish their act away from the glare of publicity. It also ensured they would actually make some money out of their playing. At the regular rock venues, it was not unusual for a support

Y o u n g

Paul with:
top left: John Taylor
below left: Little Richard
below: Helen Slater

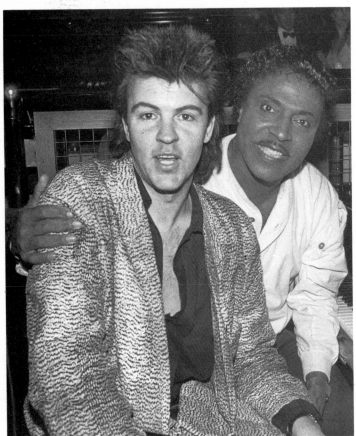

22

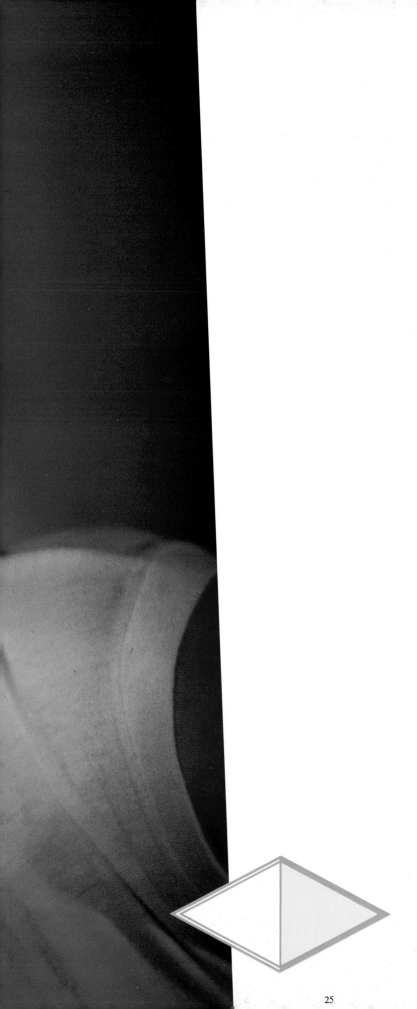

band to be paid just £5 for their performance, both band and club management assuming that the prestige of playing these places far outweighed financial considerations. Plus, you had more chance of being seen by press and record companies at the Marquee than you did playing a tiny pub in Neasden.

Street Band, however, regularly earned £10 a night each from their pub gigs. It was money well earned. On some nights they were terrified and they were often forced to play simply to stop the audience from rioting! Their policy was simple. If the crowd didn't want to enjoy themselves, it was the band's job to make them. It wasn't unusual for Paul to spend most of his time swearing at the audience, doing anything to attract their attention for the next song. One of their weapons in this fight was a song called "Toast". It developed originally as a way of filling time while John Gifford changed his guitar strings. Paul began by telling the crowd about the delights of eating toast and the rest of the group just picked it up from there, playing along and shouting out "Toast" every time Paul mentioned the word. John Gifford later claimed that "the song was going to be called 'Spunk' but that didn't seem commercially viable, so we retitled it."

Street Band spent much of the summer of '78 touring with The Movies then, in August, went into the studio to record their first single. They were produced by Chas Jankel, one time member of Ian Dury's Blockheads, and it was he who suggested Street Band record "Toast". They finished the song which was to be the A-side of the single, the breezy "Hold On", but their attempts at recording a B-side all met with failure. So, with three hours of studio time remaining, work began on "Toast".

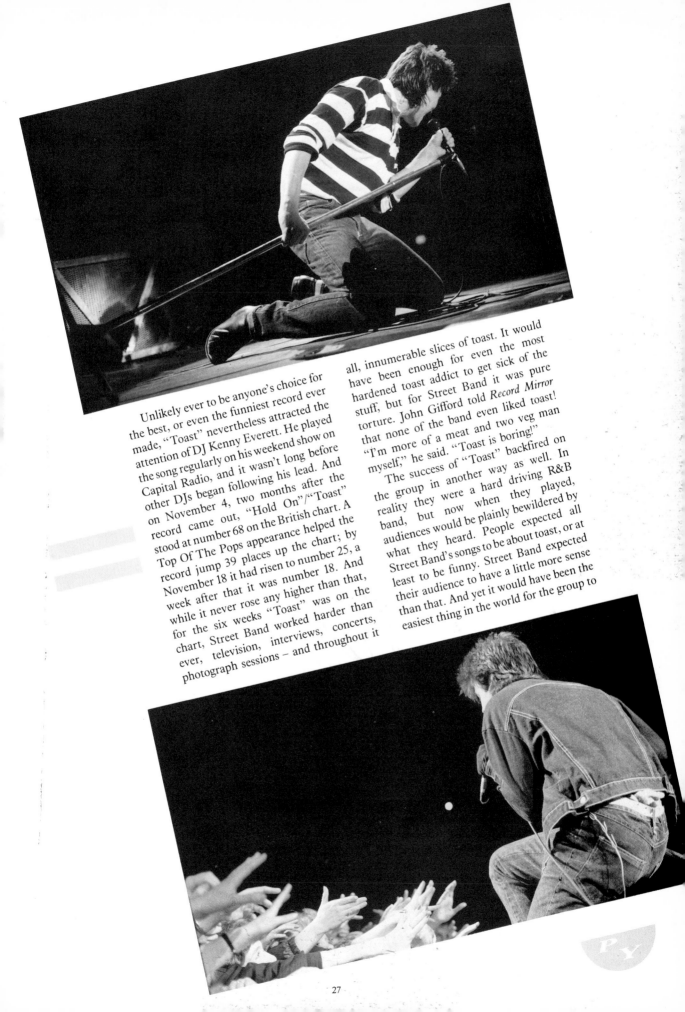

Unlikely ever to be anyone's choice for the best, or even the funniest record ever made, "Toast" nevertheless attracted the attention of DJ Kenny Everett. He played the song regularly on his weekend show on Capital Radio, and it wasn't long before other DJs began following his lead. And on November 4, two months after the record came out, "Hold On"/"Toast" stood at number 68 on the British chart. A Top Of The Pops appearance helped the record jump 39 places up the chart; by November 18 it had risen to number 25, a week after that it was number 18. And while it never rose any higher than that, for the six weeks "Toast" was on the chart, Street Band worked harder than ever, television, interviews, concerts, photograph sessions – and throughout it

all, innumerable slices of toast. It would have been enough for even the most hardened toast addict to get sick of the stuff, but for Street Band it was pure torture. John Gifford told *Record Mirror* that none of the band even liked toast! "I'm more of a meat and two veg man myself," he said. "Toast is boring!"

The success of "Toast" backfired on the group in another way as well. In reality they were a hard driving R&B band, but now when they played, audiences would be plainly bewildered by what they heard. People expected all Street Band's songs to be about toast, or at least to be funny. Street Band expected their audience to have a little more sense than that. And yet it would have been the easiest thing in the world for the group to

please punters and bank managers alike had they only felt inclined. Amongst the more conventional numbers in their repertoire were an over-acted version of Tom Jones' "It's Not Unusual", an absurd cover of "Shaking All Over" and a quite hysterical ode to the joys of making love in a mini-van called "Juvenile Love". The last thing they wanted, however, was to be labelled a novelty band. The second Street Band single, instead of one of their jokey numbers, was "One More Step" – a great song but miles removed from what the band's audience wanted to hear. Almost as a matter of course, "One More Step" flopped quite dismally – a fate which was shared by their third single, "Mirror Star", and the band's first LP, "London".

Part of the problem lay with the band's inability to shake off the ghost of their first hit (Paul later admitted that, if they had had any sense, the group would have insisted "Toast" be released under a false name), but also to blame was their inability to go out on tour in support of their latest records. During the recording of "Dilemma" Paul's voice simply snapped. Fortunately the damage was not serious, but it was time consuming. He submitted to an intensive vocal training course, and for a while he could only speak in whispers.

A year and two singles later their second album – "Dilemma" – was released to similar response, and as the record sank below the horizon, so did Street Band.

"I panicked for a bit," he said later. "I thought I would never be able to speak again, although in the end all it took was patience."

He lost the top octave of his voice, along with £600 in medical expenses and, he later joked, he lost his band as well. In December 1979 it was announced in the press that Street Band had broken up.

As part of his convalescence, Paul, Mick Pearl and John Gifford put together a low-key soul band, something to help pass the time and give Paul an opportunity to get back into the habit of singing. As a therapeutic remedy it was an inspired idea. As a piece of good timing it was a masterstroke. Britain, at that time, was in the grip of a Mod revival, and with it came a growing interest in the soul music of the early Sixties – precisely the same sounds as Paul had so happily grown up with. He immediately saw the chance to put the failure of Street Band behind him and set about bringing the new group's personnel up to full strength. Besides the three ex-Street Band-ers, there was keyboard player Ian "Rev" Kewley, drummer Barry Watts, trumpeter Tony Hughes and two saxophonists, Steve Farr and Stewart Blandamer. "We used to get together and jam in pubs in our spare time," Stewart told *Record Mirror*. "Then one day a guy from Virgin Records came to see us and we thought there must be something in what we were doing so we decided to go out and buy suits, do the whole thing properly. We haven't stopped working since."

Q-Tips, as the new band dubbed themselves, played their first gig at a pub near St. Albans. They made their London début at the Golden Lion, Fulham, at the end of November – before most people even knew Street Band had broken up! That venue later gave the band a weekly residency. Other early venues included the Bridgehouse in Canning Town, the 101 Club in Clapham and the Queen's Arms, Wealdstone. And out of town promoters, too, became interested. When Q-Tips played the Sheffield Limit Club, one of their first ever trips out of the Home Counties, they were greeted by an almost full house.

Having made such an impact on the live circuit, Q-Tips worked it solidly. It wasn't long before their own name began to attract far more people than the "Ex-Street Band" tag which some cautious promotors used to advertise the gigs. And as the band's reputation grew, so did their personal satisfaction. "I know it sounds strange, but it's been everyone's dream in Q-Tips to be in a really good soul band and to wear suits," Paul once said. It was fast becoming a dream come true.

In January, 1980, Q-Tips played their first major London gig, opening for The Knack at the Dominion Theatre. Two months after that, they were recording their first single, Joe Tex's "S.Y.S.L.J.F.M. (The Letter Song)" – the title actually stood for "Save Your Sweet Love Just For Me" – and their own "The Dance". The session cost just £700, a sum which was more than recouped when the single was released on the independent Shotgun label in April. It didn't chart, but it did finally bring the band to the attention of the major record companies. Within weeks, Q-Tips were signed to Chrysalis. John Gifford left the band in May, and around the same time the line-up was augmented by a three piece brass section, all previously members of Dexy's Midnight Runners. In Gifford's place came Garth Watt-Roy, from Bonnie Tyler's band, and in this form Q-Tips opened the 1980 Crystal Palace Garden Party – and ran away with every possible accolade.

Q-Tips' next single followed later that same month. As with its predecessor, it was another cover version, "Tracks Of My Tears". The song was a hit for its composer, Smokey Robinson, back in 1966, and Q-Tips version followed hot on the heels of another Robinson cover, "Tears Of A Clown", which had just helped The Beat to their first hit.

Q-Tips weren't to be so lucky, but their fantastic performance on the record set the scene perfectly for their début album, "Q-Tips", which followed in July. This was a hit, albeit only a minor one, but there again, Q-Tips never considered themselves as potential chart-toppers. They were essentially a concert band and they proved this throughout the summer.

Initial plans to stage a complete soul revue, a whistlestop package of four or five of the best new soul bands, fell through; instead the group embarked on a lengthy tour of conventional clubs which was transformed, midway through, into the 'Buckets & Spades' tour as the band took their stage show out to the seaside resorts. They also played the Montreux Festival in

July, the Rotterdam New Pop festival in September, undertook a massive autumn tour of the U.K. and, to celebrate their first full year together, wound 1980 up with a Christmas tour with free admission to anybody who turned up dressed as the Christmas fairy!

The band later revealed that, apart from the fact they all enjoyed touring so much, one of the main reasons they did work so much was that it would've cost them money to stop! They discovered that it worked out considerably cheaper if they hired their P.A. system by the year, rather than by the night. But the saving was only appreciable if they kept working. As it was, they certainly did get their money's worth. By the end of the band's career, in September 1982, it was estimated that they had played an average of five gigs a week, every week, for the last three years. They were also the highest-paid, highest-drawing non-chart band in the United Kingdom; even when Chrysalis dropped the group from their roster in May 1981 and the band found themselves without a record contract, their success on the concert circuit showed no signs of falling away. If anything, it actually increased!

On August 1, midway through another tour, Q-Tips recorded their performance at Nottingham Theatre Royal for a live album. A second show, at the London Marquee on September 20, was also taped, but only one of the songs was intended for the LP. This was "Raise Your Hand", a song which had been an American hit for Eddie Floyd in 1967.

And the special guest vocalist on Q-Tips' version was Floyd himself!

To the band and their followers, this must have seemed the ultimate endorsement of their endeavours, but record companies were not impressed. A year after the album was originally recorded, it finally appeared in the shops, the first release on the Rewind label – a low budget concern set up by the same people as had masterminded the Shotgun company two years previous.

Throughout the confusing months of 1982 Q-Tips' manager Ged Doherty discovered that while no record company was interested in taking on Q-Tips, several suggested that Paul strike out as a solo artist. Paul's immediate response was to completely ignore the proposals. But as time went by, and still Q-Tips were no closer to landing a major record deal, he began to reconsider his position. And in December 1982, it was announced that the Q-Tips would fold, playing out with a string of farewell shows at the London Venue.

Paul signed to CBS in the autumn of 1982, at a time when the label's fortunes were at an uncharacteristically low point. Adam Ant, ruler of the roost for so long, had been dethroned; now it was Boy George and Duran Duran whose record company staff had to fight their way through the gold discs to get at their desks. A year of hits for CBS had seen only Marvin Gaye, Julio Iglesias and Nicole début on the label, none of whom seemed particularly well qualified to inspire mass teenage adulation.

It is doubtful that anybody at CBS saw Paul as the artist who would fill the gap. In fact, as Paul has said on numerous occasions, the company weren't even sure what they wanted to do with him. "They were confused about my direction," Paul said. "I think they had it in mind to push me in a lightweight, poppy soul direction."

He, however, had other ideas. He told the company he wanted to record more substantial material, and began checking out tapes sent in by various publishing companies. "They seemed to see me as the new Cliff Richard or Shaking Stevens," he said, grimacing as he remembered one company offering him Pat Benatar's "Hit Me With Your Best Shot"!

Paul's first trip to the recording studio produced three songs which, by their very diversity, gave a hint of things to come. Rather than record any of his own songs (he had seven of them) he chose "Iron Out The Rough Spots", "Love Of The Common People" and – in a move guaranteed to attract controversy – Joy Division's "Love Will Tear Us Apart".

Laurie Latham, Paul's new producer, suggested the song; Paul was uncertain at first, but eventually gave in. "I did 'Love Will Tear Us Apart' because it's a good song and I knew people would not like hearing me do it. I never stuck my neck out in Q-Tips because it was too democratic. So this time I wanted to try something a bit more bold."

He admitted that many people took Joy Division very seriously, "and are a bit upset that someone like me should do one of their songs," and for that reason he refused to allow CBS to release it as his first single. "If it's an album track people can take it or leave it. But if you put it out as a single, you're throwing it in their faces a bit. I feel quite adamant about that," he said, although he did allow the song to come out as a 45 on the Continent. Not surprisingly, it was a massive hit.

His first British single was released in November, 1982. "Iron Out The Rough Spots" passed by unnoticed by most people, the same fate which befell the follow-up, "Love Of The Common People". At this point, people began suggesting to Paul that he try working with a more experienced producer than Laurie Latham. Paul refused, telling everyone that he believed he and Laurie were on the verge of creating something big. The pressure was taken off, and CBS granted the pair one more chance. It was a wise decision.

"I was so sure 'Wherever I Lay My Hat' wasn't going to be a hit," Paul told the *New Musical Express*. "I thought 'Love Of The Common People' had been a really good single and I just couldn't understand why it failed. There was everything in there, nice playing, a good arrangement, and I didn't overplay the part of being a singer." Yet the song flopped.

"Wherever I Lay My Hat" remained at number one throughout the summer of 1983, one of the best selling singles of the year. Paul's début LP "No Parlez" echoed the success, while the tour which Paul and The Royal Family undertook that autumn sold out in next to no time. Two triumphant nights in London rounded off the outing; from there Paul and his girlfriend took off for Paradise Island, in the Bahamas, for an idyllic holiday surrounded by what Paul later described as "Palm trees, blue seas, white sands and useless nightlife".

A short promotional tour of the United States was next on the agenda. "Wherever I Lay My Hat" had just been released there and Paul faced five days of being shuttled from one hotel room to another, giving interviews to both the American and English press, and bemoaning his absence from home. "I bought a flat in Highgate and got the keys the same week as 'Wherever I Lay My Hat' got to number 1. I moved all my stuff in, but since then I've only just managed to get it all out of the boxes. I've only got half the carpets down. It's ridiculous!"

"Wherever I Lay My Hat" surprisingly failed to make the American chart and so, in the New Year, Paul and The Royal Family returned for an eight city tour. This time around they were rewarded when "Come Back And Stay", already a Top 3 hit in the UK, reached the American Top 30.

Back in Britain, little had been heard of Paul since December. In that month a reissue of "Love Of The Common People" gave him his third successive smash hit, an extensive television advertising campaign ensured that "No Parlez" filled enough Christmas stockings to keep it on top of the album chart and Paul's Christmas Eve show at the Hammersmith Odeon, the last date of his 12 Days Of Christmas tour, was broadcast live on television and radio. Silence followed, but the various charts which music papers

Paul with Alison Moyet

with Daryl Hall

P a u l   Y o u n g

and their readers delight in compiling every New Year showed that Paul had not been forgotten. "No Parlez" made the Best Album category in all the music papers and *Sounds* and *NME* both placed him as 1983's ninth Best New Artist. In the Best Vocalist section he finished third in both *NME* and *Smash Hits*, beating even David Bowie and Michael Jackson. *NME* readers even voted him the seventh Best Dressed Man of the year. And, just to prove that Paul Young had really arrived, he even scraped into the Creep and Wally Of The Year categories, behind the usual selection of twisted politicians, addle-brained journalists and obstreperous media darlings. It was all a very far cry from just twelve months before, when Paul had been reading the poll results and "Wishing I could be in there."

With tours of Europe, Japan, Australia and America under their belts, as well as a prestigious headline position at the annual CBS convention in Hawaii, Paul and The Royal Family returned home in June 1984 to play the 3rd Annual Prince's Trust Rock Gala, at the Royal Albert Hall. They topped a bill which also featured Sade and Imagination, and the celebrity packed audience included the Prince and Princess of Wales, patrons of the Trust. That same month it was announced that "No Parlez", which had already won Paul a gold disc in November, was now certified triple platinum – a fine way to celebrate a full fifty-two weeks on the chart. It topped the chart in Britain on three separate occasions and on the Continent it had been number one in a dozen other countries.

It was only days after the Prince's Trust concert that Paul contracted a throat virus which, temporarily, caused him to lose half a dozen notes from the middle range of his voice. It was a heavy blow, which apart from necessitating daily visits to a voice specialist, also robbed Paul and the band of two further major concert appearances. The first was a headlining spot on the Channel 4 programme A Midsummer Night's Tube; the other was a place on the bill of Elton John's "Summer Of '84" concert at Wembley Stadium.

It was a heavy blow, but it left Paul with a little more time in which to plan his next trip to the recording studio. And at the end of August, the papers were able to announce Paul's complete recovery from the virus.

"It was an absolutely horrifying experience. I'd had a few days off and was sitting at home when I thought it would be a good idea to get in a bit of practice. So I got out the guitar and started playing . . . but I just couldn't sing. I could only go so far up the range, then it was like hitting a wall. I couldn't go a note higher. I tried absolutely everything to get my voice working – exercise, drugs to relax the throat muscles, even steroids to try and clear up the problem. I was in an absolute frenzy, trying to get it working."

As a last resort, Paul went to see his doctor. And was told that the best thing he could do was go on holiday – and get drunk! "He's a good bloke, my doctor. But it didn't make me feel any better. You can say the last year hasn't been the best of my life."

In September, Paul's vinyl silence was broken with the release of a new single, the powerful "I'm Gonna Tear Your Playhouse Down", a song Paul originally heard being sung by Ann Peebles. "We've reshuffled the words a bit to give it a slightly more political edge rather than leave it with the usual lover connotations. This isn't me getting on the politics bandwagon, I just wanted a change."

A change in lyrical bias was accompanied by a change in the stage-show. The Fabulous Wealthy Tarts, the two girls whose distinctive backing vocals had lent so much to "No Parlez" and the ensuing tours, opted out of accompanying The Royal Family on further live outings. But for Paul, his lifestyle continued much the same way as it had since his early days with Kat Kool. No sooner was his recovery announced than a British tour was set up, a thirteen date outing which culminated in two highly over-subscribed nights at the massive Wembley Arena.

Back in September, Paul admitted that British fans were unlikely to be seeing much of him over the next twelve months. His goal for 1985 was to finally conquer America. "I think they're fools over there for not having caught onto it yet as much as they should have done," he said. "I'm now an 'underground' success in the States, and I think it's pretty cool to know me at the moment. 'Come Back And Stay' got in the Top 30 but even so, in America that only means an extra ten people come to your gigs. Over there, popularity has nothing to do with hit singles – it's about albums and 'credibility', whatever that is. Like The Police, I suppose."

Twelve months after those remarks, Paul had both credibility and a popular album. "The Secret Of Association", his second solo set, was released in March – an instant British success and almost as swiftly, an American hit as well. With it came a further two hit singles as well; in December, one of Paul's own compositions, the yearning "Everything Must Change", reached the Top 10; four months later, his cover of Daryl Hall and John Oates' "Every Time You Go Away" did likewise on both sides of the Atlantic Ocean. Simultaneously, Paul and The Royal Family embarked on a six month world tour covering the U.K., Europe, Australia, Japan and the United States, playing in front of some of the largest – and most adoring – audiences they had ever seen. In fact, on July 13, they appeared in front of *the* largest audience; onstage at Wembley Stadium, Paul's three song set was seen by millions of homes around the world as he joined in the all-star cavalcade which culminated some

eight months of work on the part of the Band Aid organisation. Paul's vocal performance on the "Do They Know It's Christmas" single has often been described as one of the stand-out moments on that particular record; at Live Aid he turned in a duet with Alison Moyet, on "That's The Way Love is", which positively dwarfed most of the afternoon's other acts.

1985 wound up with what has become a tradition for Paul – a Christmas tour of the United Kingdom. By the time it reached its conclusion, spread over so many triumphant nights in the capital, Paul Young had achieved more in just three years than many people can fit into their entire lives. He is a superstar the world over. He has, thanks to Princess Diana's oft-professed admiration for his talents, won even Royal approval. There can be few goals left for this 29-year-old son of a Luton factory worker to attain, and even were his entire career to collapse tomorrow, Paul would be left with few regrets. "I only ever wanted to be a singer," he says. "I can't think of doing anything apart from singing. If I wasn't doing that, I would probably be playing Russian roulette." He has described singing as his vocation, which he believes is something every singer must feel (but which, in reality, very few really seem to).

"It has to be in your blood. I always felt that I had something. I always knew what made people good. I knew what made Jagger good, I knew what made Bowie good, I knew what made James Brown good. And I always felt that I was learning the right lessons from watching those people.

"When I heard other people talking about their heroes, I could never tell what they were going on about. I could always tell that they were on the wrong path. (But) I was very sure what I wanted, all the way."

As the 1980s pass their half-way mark, he would seem to have got it.

P a u l   Y o u n g

discography

STREET BAND singles

September 1978: Hold On/Toast *Logo GO 325*
October 1978: Toast/Hold On (reversed and repromoted) *Logo GO 325*
January 1979: One More Step/Things Are Never Quite What They Seem *Logo GO 341*
March 1979: Love Sign/Loud Music *Logo GO 348*
August 1979: One Good Reason/Happy Families *Logo GO 356*
October 1979: Mirror Star/It Takes A Thief *Logo GO 368*

STREET BAND albums

February 1979: London *Logo 1012*
October 1979: Dilemma *Logo 1017*
1984: Street Band Featuring Paul Young *Cambra CR 140*

Q-TIPS singles

April 1980: S.Y.S.L.J.F.M./The Dance *Shotgun SHOT 1*
June 1980: Tracks Of My Tears/Different World *Chrysalis CHS 2420*
September 1980: A Man Can't Lose/Some Kinda Wonderful *Chrysalis CHS 2456*
April 1981: Stay The Way You Are/Sweet Talk/Looking For Some Action *Chrysalis CHS 2518*
October 1981: Love Hurts/I Wish It Would Rain *Rewind 10*
May 1982: You Are The Life Inside Of Me/Raise Your Hand *Rewind 11*
July 1982: Love Hurts/You're Gonna Love Me *Rewind 15*
July 1984: You Are The Life Inside Of Me/Love Hurts/I Wish It Would Rain/Hi Fidelity *Rewind 19*

Q-TIPS albums

August 1980: Q-Tips *Chrysalis CHR 1255*
June 1982: Live At Last *Rewind RELP 100*
October 1983: Q-Tips Featuring Paul Young *Fame 3087*
1984: Live At Last: Q-Tips Featuring Paul Young *Rewind RELP 1001*

PAUL YOUNG singles

November 1982: Iron Out The Rough Spots/Behind Your Smile *CBS A2751*
January 1983: Love Of The Common People/Tender Trap *CBS PY 1*
May 1983: Wherever I Lay My Hat/Broken Man *CBS A3371*
June 1983: Wherever I Lay My Hat/SEX/Broken Man *CBS A123371*
August 1983: Come Back And Stay/Yours *CBS A/A12 3636*
November 1983: Love Of The Common People/Wherever I Lay My Hat/It's Better To Have *CBS A/A12 3585*
December 1983: Love Will Tear Us Apart/One Step Forward/Come Back And Stay *German CBS A4238*
September 1984: I'm Gonna Tear Your Playhouse Down/Come Back And Stay *CBS A4766*
September 1984: I'm Gonna Tear Your Playhouse Down/Broken Man/One Step Forward *CBS TA 4766*
November 1984: Everything Must Change/Give Me My Freedom *CBS A 4972*
November 1984: Everything Must Change/Give Me My Freedom/Everything Must Change (instrumental)
   I Close My Eyes And Count To Ten *CBS DA 4972*
March 1985: Everytime You Go Away/This Means Anything *CBS A 6300*
June 1985: Tomb Of Memories/The Man In The Iron Mask *CBS A 6321*
June 1985: Tomb Of Memories/The Man In The Iron Mask/Bite The Hand/No Parlez *CBS TA 6321*

PAUL YOUNG albums

July 1983: No Parlez *CBS 25521*
March 1984: The Secret Of Association *CBS 26234*